To Izzy,

book of poems was suited to you since you're a beautiful, creative, unique writer. Remember me when you're a famous writer in NYC or LA. Love you lots.
XO,
Hannah

SOFT FOCUS

Published by Metatron
www.onmetatron.com
Montreal Québec Canada

Copyright © Sarah Jean Grimm, 2017
All rights reserved
ISBN 978-1-988355-04-7

Publisher | Ashley Opheim
Cover design | Eric Amling
Author photo | Tramaine George

First edition
First printing

We acknowledge the support of the Canada Council for the Arts, which last year invested $153 million to bring the arts to Canadians throughout the country.

Canada Council   Conseil des arts
for the Arts   du Canada

SOFT FOCUS

SARAH JEAN GRIMM

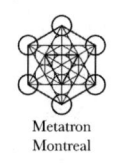

Metatron
Montreal

SOFT FOCUS

MENARCHE	1
EARLY EVOLUTION	3
STRAY BEAST	5
DIVIDE THE HOOF	7
WINNERS CIRCLE	9
HOT SPOT	11
SHAPEWEAR	13
GLAM GIRLS	17
COHABIT	20
IUD	22
CENTRAL TRUST	23
HOLOCENE	25
TOO LATE	28
NEW PYRAMID	30
COOL BLUE MIDDLES	32
LUXE CAPACITOR	35
FINAL GIRL	37
SOFT FOCUS	40
PERCEPTUAL EASE	41
SLUTSPURT	44
MANTRA	46
NAGL	47
PARTIAL THEORIES ON	48
CRYSTAL PALACE	50
AFTERGLOW	53

**WINNER OF THE
2016 METATRON PRIZE**

MENARCHE

I was born
Small and slime-covered

I found a wolf to lick me clean
Raise me wild
Enough to get me out of the woods

Nightly I pressed wheat into flat circles
Watched it bristle seedful
Potential made the best bedding

I arrived winded at the altar
Warbling my past death
My future life

I languished on a broad beach
The lesser animals I sacrificed
Bloodied in my mandibles

My bones warmed before they softened
I fevered as the moon rose

My marrow howled lupine
For an aching
Frenzied hour of what next

My danger

EARLY EVOLUTION

Be a doll now, you say, and I am become one
I pluck a flock raw for its plumage
Strip, I say, and birds strip bare
I stuff myself so full with their stuffing
I bulge with all their lorem ipsum
Poke me and I spill sawdust from featherguts
I fear everything that could happen to this form
The worst would be if you didn't notice my hunger
I could dance seven veils to thrive you
I could drive stakes into highway medians
To campaign for your attention
I would have the edge of an underdog
Underfed and unassuming
Is it beauty when it baffles you?
With the right filter I am half pretty
But mostly very ugly for my habitat
Rank me on a supersmooth bell curve
Numbers evade me so give me images
Be a doll now and bring me my silver charger
Loaded with one Star Ruby and an antique melon-baller
Self-pity is the soul of my wit, you say
But I'm working to extinguish that urge

I burn lovely hairs at my bedside
I steal fresh palms from my neighbors
And swirl these together in a saucepan
To keep the pests from coming in

STRAY BEAST

It slays me the way
You get your fix
And shove off
After I've performed me
I'd like a shower
But all my invisible contaminants
My wide-shining fears
Are stored in my fat cells
I've got so many of these
I could never
Achieve thigh gap
Or any kind of shortage
You'd like to fix
Though I am getting warmer
So bloody in my abdomen
Braying in the bathtub as
I drip hot wax on my skin
To grow younger by
I make a pact with myself
To become so garish
And well-adorned

As to be confused for beauty
As to be mounted
As to be put out to pasture
Some sunlit place
Where I can glut myself
On green things
Go so straight I'll
Only want to fuck myself

DIVIDE THE HOOF

What hurts today is the evidence of effort
I brushed my teeth and lined my eyes
Came back to bed and felt mistaken
Some days I am more synthetic than others
I have many moods
They turn in systems
I am in the habit of my own diagonals
But I get that the patterns are medley
How the sky is ugly
Even when it's not
Some days I make myself a fatted calf
Chewing cud for your arrival
How pleased I am to have you
Even as you show me the rumper
The splitter
The vat dipper
If I imagine these things are paper and gloss
I can get off on my own lack
My moods are many animals
We're all lined up at the stockyard
Waiting our turns
Some day I'd like to be

One prime cut of my choicest offering
When you eat an animal
Are you absorbing its life or its death
I'm not sure it makes a difference

WINNERS CIRCLE

This morning I said sorry to a stranger
As I cut him off on the stairs
Apology can be a form of love if it's convincing
I'm not accusing you of loving me
It's just
I'm kind of an expert on this one thing
Which is
My heat on your fingers
My hair on your clothes
My feet in your shoes
My camera in your retina
The female gaze is all about me
Looking at you
Looking at me
Which is to say
It's like the male gaze but more aware of what it's doing
We all have a role to play and this one's mine
I'm holding a mirror up to my own face
It is a convex mirror
It is such a fun glass
In it my hips look massive but my nose becomes smallish

I'm concentrating the sun's rays through the fun glass
And onto my face to impart character
A scar story for dinner parties
All my party tricks are pretty show ponies
I chronicle their victories and name them things
Magic Moment
Personal Best
Wolf Mother
Power Play
When we perform together I wear a rubber horse mask
The teeth are always baring down and gnashing
It's like I'd do anything for a carrot and some sugar
I'll take you to The Winners Circle
That's the name of a nite club uptown
But I mean it another way too

HOT SPOT

Love is not a natural beauty
Love threads its eyebrows
Lasers imperfections

If I had the capital
I could look like love
Simulacra and simulation

To get love I listen
To give love I regurgitate

Vomit implies a lack of control
But I'm talking discipline
I'm talking two fingers
Real romantic puke that says
I understand

Empathetic mirroring
A learned behavior

To be trained on approval
Is to be a girl at the turn of the century
I'm talking every century

It's easy to like
And be like
And be liked

In some of this I am I
In some of this I am or feel unruly

When you graze a pleasure center
My mind grows lizardly
I see that other me who is pleased by pleasing
Like a version

Do I feel fuller with your two fingers
Inserted liquidly
Is this feeling connecting you to me

Life is neat and comprehendible
I am I, I, I
Who could blame me for losing my senses

SHAPEWEAR

A body is matter to be molded

To make a better shape
Not some boring shrub fruit

Try an hourglass if you want to
Remind a man of his mortality
Best to become a clock

Sands of time inside you
Each time you are picked up and turned over

You will always be itching
Never mind the home remedies
Some men like to have a project
To hammer away at

Did you know some women are shaped like bananas
I have never seen one myself
In the wild

Only as Figure 3. in a state-approved textbook
Because they teach this stuff in health class
To lead girls into their own dysmorphia

You are what you eat
So from now on I am surviving on spunk
I want to possess whatever allows you to be bold
Without getting called feisty

My gut reaction when I am in the world
Is to apologize

No one's ever said sorry to me
For making my eyelashes stick together
With their egg on my face

I am doll eyes but I need a doll waist
I make a lovely figure with what I've been given
When I encase my body in exoskeleton

This is how I want
To be looked at but not seen

Who decides what the body absorbs
Versus what it reflects

And how are our bodies not
The most boring thing about us
By now

I would starve mine to transcend
Or shuffle off
If I knew you wouldn't find it cute

I would stand naked at the altar
In the name of the Patriarchy
In the name of its Sons
In the name of the Spirit of Capitalism

When can we retire the syllogism
Time is money is the root of evil

We all know that women are the root
And the dirt and the stem and the bulb

We are ripe swelling fruits
Carrying the seeds
Of our mutually assured destruction

The ways in which we fuck each other up
Let me count them
They are endless fluffy sheep
Bedding me for beauty rest

GLAM GIRLS

We have many teeth and
There is so much to be bitten and we have
Brittle bodies trying to be tiny things
It is such an effort
An exercise in avoidance
It takes the focus of all our neurons
To make these dense things light
Synapses fire and there is brightness
Our minds manufacture distractions
Levees against the pull of the gut
It is a skill
Practiced for the sake of our bodies
Demanding their very smallness
Becomes the elephant in the room

There is an island full of girls like us
We feed each other stone fruits
Grow allergies together
We make necklaces from our fallen teeth
And straws from native reeds
There is music always and everywhere
The wind rustling sweet-grass
Ocean hushing shoreline
If we lie out here long enough
The weather erodes us
Whittles our unwieldy bones
The too-bigness of being
If we soak in saltwater we shrink
Sponges set aside
Shriveled up

Our goal is to glow from the effort
Our goal is to reek of self-discipline
Our goal is to inspire destruction
Have you heard the story of Helen?
When we body this way
It is a dare
When we body this way
We say a truth and call it a lie
We want to give you only glimpses
We forbid you to peer all the way in
We are afraid you will find every answer
And move on
We are afraid you won't find any answers
And move on
We want you to move on us
Tell us we are compelling and mean it
We are magnetic like that aren't we

COHABIT

The tigers we imported

Are padding around their fresh enclosure

We've bred them to purr at a special frequency

One that reminds us of womb noises

These sounds comb our organs

Tell us our architecture is sound

We've bred them so their mouths won't water

We leave lock and key within their reach

They are happy here in their small orbits

Every day gleams within the painted fence

We enjoy the controlled climate and perennial blooms

We hold their claws against our clavicles

And nothing shatters

There is hardly anything left

I never told you

IUD

You make me feel
Like a natural woman

CENTRAL TRUST

I fashion myself a great forgiver

In the western tradition of loving

Though I would prefer to ignore

Your suitcase full of apology

Not unpack for days

And let the laundry burst

I know I should keep far from me

The impulse to water your plants

I can't hold everything I want at once

I wait for strength to take hold

In these uncertain times

As ever

It's important to be able to lift your own weight

Welcome to the era of accountability

Where you're always feeling limp and afraid

The sometimes quality of want

I totally get that

Sorry I say

Now you say sorry too

HOLOCENE

In the dream I swim in green pools
I call them California
The waters witness my vacancies

I have lied that I have none
I have lied from my deepest lung
I have lied in hot color

The waters breed gnats
to break my skin awake
The dark falls off the ledge

Into the bottom of morning
Cracks an egg in the air Hello
I am awake to the ways I can be cracked

I can be the drug of my own biology
In the dream I live inside a mouth
It keeps me humid and happy

I am the most fertile I have
the greenest scales always
on the verge of feathering

Hello chicken wing Hello
drumstick I am edible and alive but totally
incompatible with your enzymes

In the dream my body dissolves
in soft places first
I find my jaw inside the hard ground

not at all where I left it
It takes an event to crack open
I am a lost mine I come in pieces

I come to you for milk
Hello Holocene I am all over
your geography

I see your taxonomy and I raise you
this honey this hard bargain
this smoking gun this aerosol

It takes an event or just
an unsteady drip of ultraviolet
In the dream I am leaking

I swim inside the waters
I ink into them slowly
The dark sloughs off the ledge into my mouth

Milk becomes a dirty word
The wind tunnels through vacant honeycombs
The same wind combs my hair

I witness the lies
I testify on my last remaining egg
It is all I have it is too late

TOO LATE

I've got a green lawn like everybody else
My milk is fortified and certified
I've got eggs to boil
Meat to grind
I've wrung my hands around the concept of mercy
Dispatched it painlessly
It doesn't always work the first time
You need strong hands
To believe you are a better animal
It's okay to cry when you clean your plate
Oh give me the steed and the gun that I need
To render my excess to tallow
I guess it's too late to feel at home
With the full range of my emotions
I've spent mornings attempting to tenant
Whichever glad structure
I managed to raise overnight
It's okay
I'm told it's okay
I'm told I'll grow into it
By the time the scaffolding comes down
Now I cradle each tomato in the grocery aisle

Place decorative accents in the garden
Set potted plants down in the yard
I click my heels
I guess it's too late to live on the farm
To lie back in a field of a thousand wheat stalks
Pointing out clouds that look like animals living
In the sky which we act like belongs to us all

NEW PYRAMID

It's Sunday and I'm pure
My insides whiskey-rinsed
From another seven day cleanse
I walk among the people
With my fist open
With my jaw closed
Around a protein morsel
Which I've taken without asking
What is safe harbor
When sea levels are rising
Tomorrow is iridescent radar
I've seen it in a dream
Your eyes were marbled there
When I looked into them
I searched for seven continents
On which to spread my message
My untested superstitions
I wanted to gift you
Seven species of pollen
Drizzled honey
An inoculation
Such is the purity of my intention

Is it religious
The way I restrict myself
With my nails clipped
With my ankles crossed
Is it religious is there incense
Leaking out of this poem
I think a universal thought
As if I could be a blank mind
Washed against a sea of whatever

COOL BLUE MIDDLES

If it were summer, we'd be cruising the internet

For an affordable car to take to the beach

Where we'd unfold lawn chairs and bite into limes

Or else I'd fish a coin out of a mall fountain

And deposit it in a glacial lake

I think wishes should come

From the cool blue middles of things

I'm worn with longing

The object of affection is always absent

Or whatever it was Kant said in that other time

There's a different heat to the planet now

Radiation grains us into truer people

We can't sustain a super flared enthusiasm

And I support a gradual dissolve into an unfazed aesthetic

A studied monotony voiced from the edges

I wish to extract myself from the messes of other people

There are many kinds of wars going on

All at once and in terrible concert

Outrage burns itself out and reignites

A closed loop of fuzzy logic

Called the web

Note the magic absent from my morning's Craigslist ad:

Seeking Master of Tarot to Write Deck

The mechanical advice in my afternoon clickbait:

Practice on Light Switch to Improve Cunnilingus

Which recalls for me that Plath line:

Darling, all night I have been flickering off, on, off, on

I don't know if she was imagining then

What I'm imagining now

But granting any kind of wish is a blue ribbon endeavor

And you should understand

In knowing what I want

I already have what I want

LUXE CAPACITOR

When they told me I was a witch
I believed them

I started stripping layers
to stay afloat

I liked to give the people
what they wanted

Approval powdered me
a milky Victorian

I could feed the whole village
on the whites of my eyes

with my meanest look
If I smiled I threatened pearls

my mouth an oyster
open for irritants

For maximum loveliness I tried just
a suggestion of suction

I drooled on my mirror
and nearly drowned

I grew these warts for my own sake
baked my skin on terracotta tiles

Shimmer and matte
powered my hold

their thickest polymers
couldn't hold me

FINAL GIRL

I played a dead girl on TV

in order to preserve my bloom

I studied the abrupt edge of youth

so I could get the petal just right

Lilies of the valley girdling our yearbook photos

See how fertile we still can be?

How conspicuous in our arrangements?

I had myself twenty angels given me this morning

Our Laura Palmers, Rosie Larsens, et al, et al

In my own limelight

Did I want to start or end up dead?

The formula went Sex = Death

Solve for virgin, solve for whore

I thought I'd like to be a Final Girl

driving some pointed object through the killer's soft bits

but as soon as I felt the pleasure of relief

I had to be punished

Enjoyment in the act of retribution was not for me

When we finished filming

I had myself a Viking funeral

I sailed above my body

for the clearest view of its destruction

I'd learned my part thoroughly

Everyone remains convinced

SOFT FOCUS

I find myself sometimes existing in sections
I can't seem to pick a face and stick with it
Did you know that if you make yourself
smile when you are sad,
you will actually become happier?
The body reinforces the brain
If I make myself smile
when I am told to smile,
is that the patriarchy making me happier?
The world fatigues me in this way
and in others
If you call it a detox instead of a diet,
no one questions your motives
There are women losing water weight
by wrapping sections of their bodies in plastic
I practice myself plastic and my lips crack
But the right shade of foundation still coheres me
I can seem even-tempered
if I am a frosted cake
I'm painting my nails the color of rice
A book I read and loved told me
eat rice have faith in women
And that's what I'm trying to do

PERCEPTUAL EASE

The zodiac says I'm suited for commerce

Scratching a semiotic itch

My late capitalist compulsions

My urges to participate

I want the stars to act on me

I'm bloated with the fantasies I project

A sense of quiet pleasure

Followed by a depression

Is fallow ground for a pure condition

To take over for good

Existence is a compromise

An agreed upon reality

Upheld by ceremony

I pledge allegiance to my selves

I find some evidence of me in every mirror

I take beauty personally

The stagnant wealth of it

And its uneven distribution

But I regret confusing the ordinary

For the sublime

That cognitive bias

Known as the halo effect

It's a lazy heuristic obstructing the truth

I've learned to see through it as social currency

But I enjoy the weight of the coin in my palm

I get it

Celebrity is the only apotheosis possible in America

When I want to engage with culture

I have to be legible in a common tongue

I have to disrupt a psychic vision

I shop with confidence

Cheap lace and black organza

I remember my training

Some consumer

SLUTSPURT

The only growth industry is suffering
Locate a life hack for the problems of culture
And you will become rich enough
To live outside the culture
With a desert island playlist
And a lifetime supply of items you desire
Enough to keep you occupied
Survival Guide: Compatibility Quiz: Aptitude Test:
What you should do for a living is try to live
Yet make it look effortless and urgent
Use words like now, hurry, and instant
This offer is good as long as supplies last
Yes, but is there something else I can do
To summon a lean season
Scarce are my urges to be contained
I've been reciting my lines
I've been minding the rules
Navigating intellectual property
In a public domain
One week into my new job
On the phone I was told I sounded twelve
Esophageal uptalk I struggle to suppress

It's a symptom of the American dream
It's the dream of a self-made supermodel
I've been searching for something I can contain
Yes, I wish to understand
Yes, I wish to continue
I wish to be less a product of internet culture
See: the stooped neck of the iPhone era
The poor posture of the navel gazer
Dread of missing out brings me up at night
Dread of pretending, dread of sincerity
Dread of being heard, dread of the banshee
Just how stupid do you think I am
Or what can I even ask
The call is coming from inside the house
Still, dread of being locked outdoors

MANTRA

I've subscribed to a meditation newsletter
for the big mistake makers. It will address a
range of my bad habits, my GMO insides,

my mainly-starch meals. I will need to fix
anything that isn't a complex-kick-ass problem.
I will need a kick-ass mantra that isn't too

complex. I will need to happen to find money
when I clean my apartment. I will need to find energy
to clean my apartment. I am trying. Can money be

trying too? I am turning off lights as I leave
rooms and timing my showers. I am cooking
at home, ordering in less, & eating to fight.

The newsletter guru says I need to be a beam
inside my own contraption. I am seeking pink
insulation that won't splotch my skin. I will

need to operate my machine with less guilt and
fewer gadgets. If I time my breathing just right,
I will find a gaggle of gods on my side.

NAGL

One way to spoil the present is to write it down
for example
I don't want to put in a poem the fact
that I'm wearing a new dress
and that I bought it for you
or that your apartment tinged pink in the evening
air thick from our shower
is where my mind goes when it needs some dopamine
or that you look supremely cute
walking through the park in your hangover shades
that the weather is oppressively hot and so are you
these surges of unqualified positive emotion
in which you have no downside
don't scare me so much as
have me thinking
I should wait until it's over
before I confess
I really liked you
in your stained blazer
in your kitchen
handing me a cigarette from your freezer
pleasurable images recurring like gifs

PARTIAL THEORIES ON

The language of

possession Something

about holding and being

held and holding a being

together Something about

bodies in motion staying

that way and one thing

that is sad to think is that

they won't really This body

and that body will be new

bodies in a decade every atom

replaced and unremembering

What law is there to make

that okay Something about

renewal We become something

new every day and maybe

there's promise in that

in not being bound to

anything but decay and

these very small things

striving for valency reaching

sometimes so hard they pull

themselves apart

CRYSTAL PALACE

I don't believe in a religion
without commerce
heavenly merchandise

but I furnish myself with myths
like the idea of my mobility
making me a good American

or the capacity of ritual
to vanish my body
into a temporary grace

I practice good posture
for lengthening stretches of time
pretending against gravity

let's pretend you're falling
for me and let's pretend
I'm not going to let you

in truth when I'm with you I feel
like I've never let anyone down
like a new president

like a royal subject
in the purple room of our enjoyment
I use my hands another way

with you watching over
performing for the archives
personal highlight reel

This morning I invented
a future which any day now
I will enter

and I surprised myself
declaring that I've been happy
for my longest stretch

this new mood a steady lamplight
I can hold inside my fist
I carry my sigil

into the crystal palace
where I can focus
on internal order and how

when I am close to you
I am closer to everything
a real citizen of the universe

next to the small animals
with their large fears
inside a canyon inside a cocoon

which everything with a molecule
has at one time touched
there must be ten thousand touches

inside your touch
like that
right there

AFTERGLOW

I got so wild that I cut a deer down

Gave it a halo when I ate it before my

Beaming TV

All these nervous tics

My fingers are clasped and I'm

Texting in tongues

I make a church with my hands and

I fill it with people

They wave at me as if to say

There's room for one more

Lamb bodies spin on a spit outside

And we shear them for sandwiches

The chickens lose their heads

They get so blissed when the blade lands

If I can hear their gutterals

I have to save them

I save them as a series of zeroes and ones

I save them by building them a website

I call it www.nothingdiesthatneverlived.com

I take an animal into my lab

Study it under fluorescence

Start a data collection

I am so gutted to know the animal

Uses every part of the animal

I keep tabs

On our apocalyptic prospects

I have several offers for after and I will be

Generous with excess

I will hold a great auction

Raffle off all-inclusives so nobody's left behind

Post-body, we are all

Glowing phosphates

There is no more mouthing will you love us

will you love us for how long

No more using our mouths to enthrall

No more lapping up dogma

Now bless me with iron and Splenda

I want to be so oversaturated with minerals

I want to glow hardest

Blink last

God, I was so bored before I got born

acknowledgments

I am grateful to the editors of the following publications for their support of individual poems in this collection: *The Atlas Review, Barrow Street, Cosmonauts Avenue, H_NGM_N, ILK, Jellyfish, The Lifted Brow, Prelude, Seizure, Similar:Peaks::, Sixth Finch, Swarm,* & *Word Riot.*

My love and thanks to Eric Amling, Naima Coster, Zoe Dzunko, Chelsea Hodson, and Ashley Opheim.

Sarah Jean Grimm is a founding editor of *Powder Keg Magazine*. She lives in Brooklyn.

When I was a kid, my favorite ice cream flavor was the one called 'rainbow.' What I most liked about the flavor wasn't its sweetness, which was like bubblegum made of strawberries and blackberries, but rather its abundance of bright colors, which, spoonful by spoonful, lick by lick, mixed until they merged.

Melted rainbow ice cream wasn't made of a thousand colors any longer, but rather only one: purple, muted, and dark; and yet, its flavor continued to be exactly the same as before.

I believe that this is precisely what happens with the poetry of Sarah Jean Grimm. Her verses are explosions of color, but they can also become a melody bitter and black. Whoever dares to read them—to lick them, to chew them—will understand that the sorrow they sometimes contain balances the sweetness of their pleasure. Thus, Soft Focus *is like a rainbow. Like a memory of childhood that flickers out. Like a magical, impossible flavor that, without doubt, will turn us into addicts.*

- LUNA MIGUEL, author of *Los estómagos*